# MORE SILHOUETTES

## 868 Copyright-Free Illustrations for Artists and Craftsmen

Edited by
Carol Belanger Grafton



DOVER PUBLICATIONS, INC.
NEW YORK

# PUBLISHER'S NOTE

The silhouette is a form of representation that has been used by many cultures throughout history—from Paleolithic times, the ancient Greeks and the Chinese of the Tang Dynasty down to such modern illustrators as Arthur Rackham. Silhouettes are prized by current artists and designers for their crispness and wit, and for the innumerable uses to which they can be put. Following on the success of her first anthology, *Silhouettes* (Dover 23781-8), Carol Belanger Grafton here presents a wide-ranging and diversified selection (incorporating new subjects such as circus, military, professions, music and transportation) assembled from sources as varied as *Fliegende Blätter*, *Punch*, *Puck*, *Harper's Weekly*, Rackham's *Midsummer Night's Dream*, and the Hawtin Engraving Company Catalogue.

# CONTENTS






Published in Canada by General Publishing Company, Ltd., 30 Lesmill Road, Don Mills, Toronto, Ontario.
Published in the United Kingdom by Constable and Company, Ltd.

*More Silhouettes: 868 Copyright-Free Illustrations for Artists and Craftsmen*, is a new work, first published by Dover Publications, Inc., in 1982.


DOVER *Pictorial Archive* SERIES




Manufactured in the United States of America
Dover Publications, Inc.
31 East 2nd Street
Mineola, N.Y. 11501

Library of Congress Cataloging in Publication Data

Main entry under the title: More Silhouettes.

1. Silhouettes. I. Grafton, Carol Belanger.
NC910.M65 741.7 81-17361 ISBN 0-486-24256-0 (pbk.) AACR2

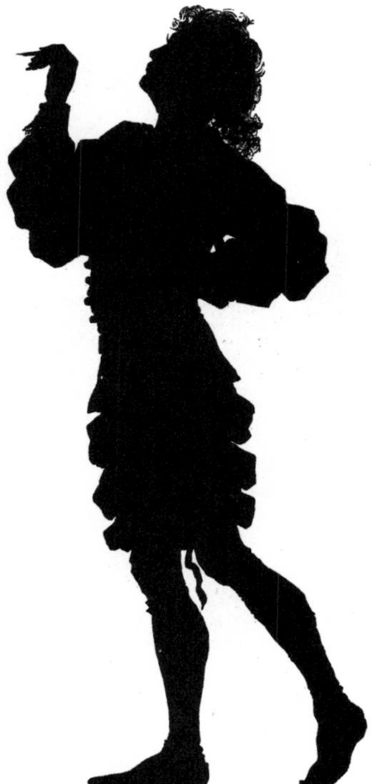

8

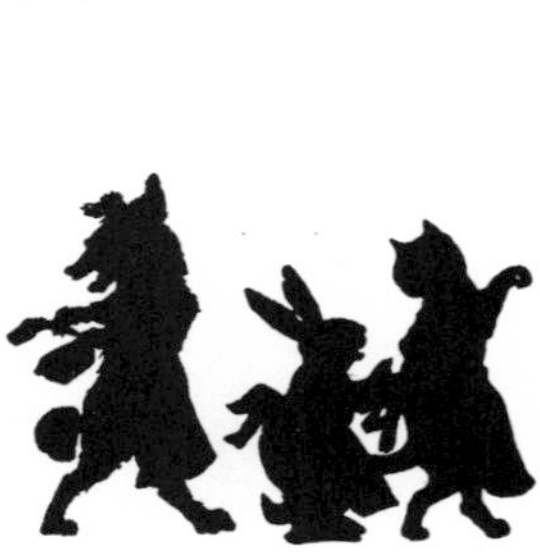

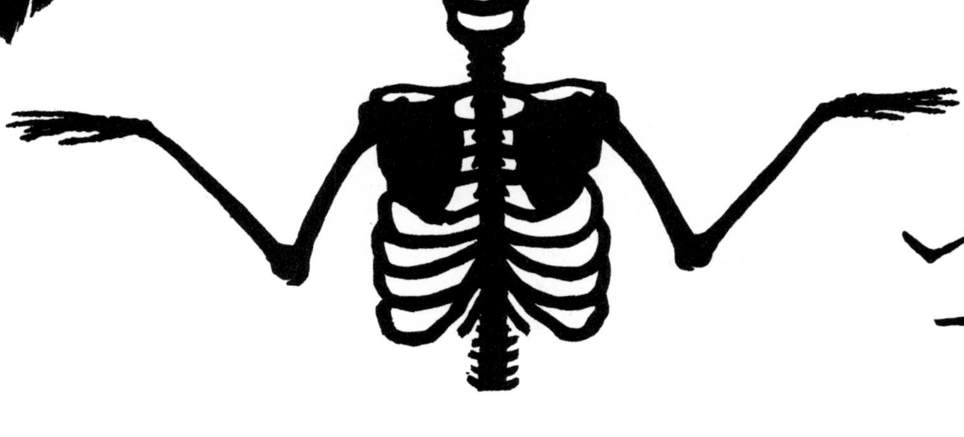

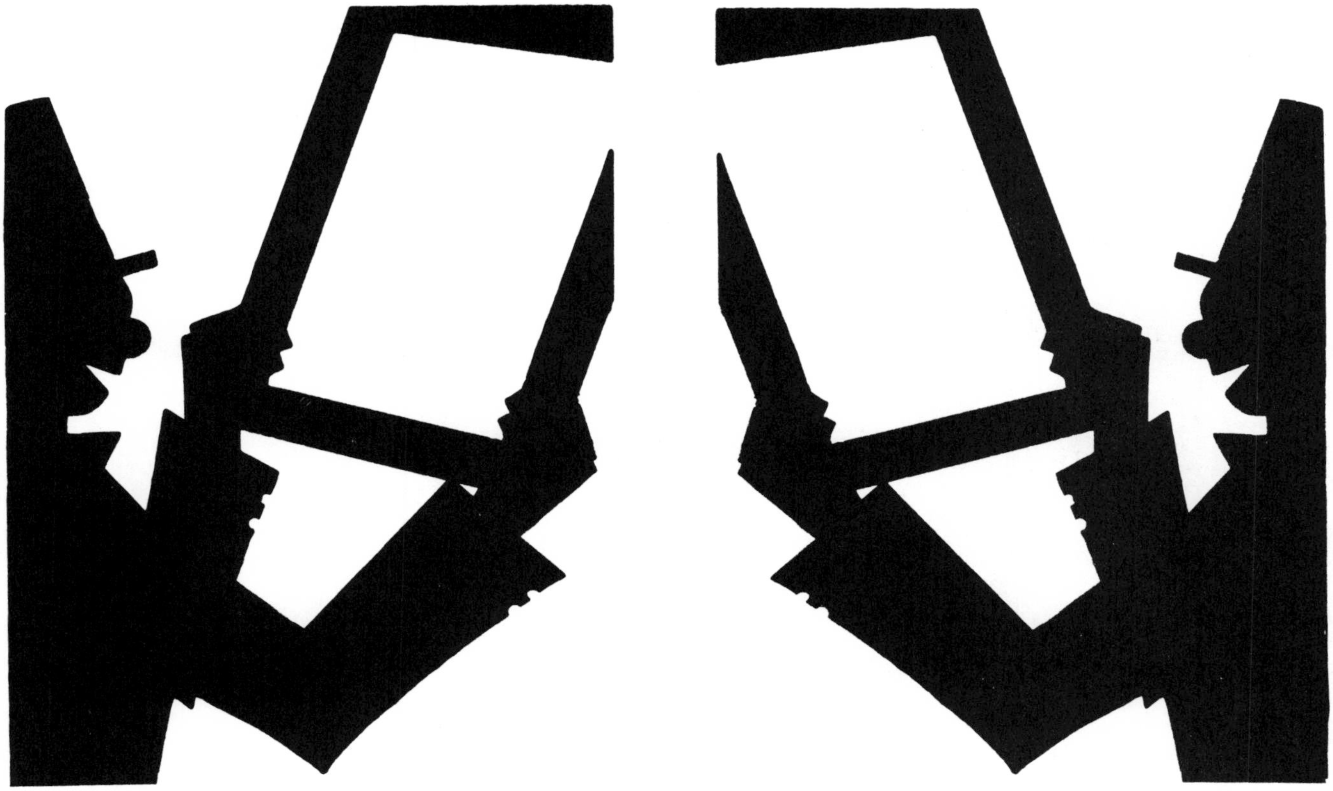